WRESTLING LI PO FOR THE REMOTE

WRESTLING LI PO FOR THE REMOTE

POEMS BY

KEVIN STEIN

FIFTH STAR PRESS
CHICAGO

Published in 2013.
Printed in the United States on acid-free paper.

Fifth Star Press
1333 West Devon Avenue, Suite 221
Chicago, Illinois 60660
Distributed by Small Press United.

20 19 18 17 16 15 14 13   1 2 3 4 5

ISBN: 9780984651054

For Deb,
    always

CONTENTS

1

Field Guide   5
Apple Blossoms at Petal-Fall with Li Po   7
April Ode to a Petunia That Outlived Winter   8
The Good Dog's Valentine Cento   9
6 Chair's Lift Line, Breckenridge   11
Upon Seeing, in Shadow, a Red Tail Hawk Plunder the Song Bird's Nest   12
Antiphon for Les Paul   13
Son Room   15
Night Visit to the Recycling Center, a Three-Album Box Set   16
Parable of the Sentence   17
Ars Poetica @ 59   19

2

Ballad of Trouvadore   25
Opening the Washing Machine's New Burstless Hoses, Made in China,
     I Think of   31
Blind Voyeur   32
Sputnik Summer   34
Forgiven   36
On the Merits of Graduate Education   38
Special Olympics   39
Parable of the Narrative   41
To Illinois's Gold Star Mothers, Who Lost a Child to War   44
In the Interest of Brevity, Let's Begin at the End   45

3

The Afterlife   49

Today I Was Happy, So I Made This Poem   50

Cardinal Numbers: Sequence in which No One Dies   52

Endnotes to the Poem "Touch" Lost with a Crashed Hard Drive   55

Sunrise, Snowfall, Two Crows among Lodgepole Pines   56

33rd Anniversary of Yard Sale Romance   57

Immigrant Song   58

In Heaven   59

Rehearsal   61

In the Name of Names   62

Pilgrim Fortune   64

Wet Carpet Awakening   66

4

Wrestling Li Po for the Remote   71

Arts Elevated and Other   73

A Brief History of History   75

Keeping Score   76

Ode to Candy Barr, Fifties' Stag Queen   79

Cat Church Communion   80

Is Beautiful   82

Parable of America in Four-Part Harmony   84

   1 / The Soup Compromise

   2 / Negotiating the Global Economy

   3 / T P

   4 / Organizational Theory

Workers on the Fifth Street Overpass   93

Chaung-tzu dreams he's a butterfly,
and a butterfly becomes Chaung-tzu.
—Li Po, "Ancient Song"

Young tree, unburdened
By anything but your beautiful natural blossoms
And dew, the dark
Blood in my body drags me
Down with my brother.

— James Wright, "To a Blossoming Pear Tree"

ALSO BY KEVIN STEIN

POETRY
Wrestling Li Po for the Remote
Sufficiency of the Actual
American Ghost Roses
Chance Ransom
Bruised Paradise
A Circus of Want

CHAPBOOKS
The Figure Our Bodies Make
A Field of Wings

CRITICISM / ESSAYS
Poetry's Afterlife: Verse in the Digital Age
Private Poets, Worldly Acts
James Wright: The Poetry of a Grown Man

ANTHOLOGIES
Bread & Steel, audio CD
Illinois Voices, edited with G. E. Murray

WRESTLING LI PO FOR THE REMOTE

I

Field Guide

If it's all about milk, it's a Lyric.

Say there's a cow lolling in green pasture,
an alliterative Angus among alfalfa,
a barbwire fence and the bull who ballsy jumps it,
he as brusque as the deed's knock-kneed calf.
That there's a Narrative poem.

If there's a lot of colloquial moo-mooing
with a touch of menace, it's Robert Frost.

The one beginning "How now brown cow"
makes fine Children's Verse.

If the cow runs with a bad herd, carrying her tail
a little too high thus breeding trouble,
it's Young Adult—
burgeoning middle school market
ripe for the poet not writing poetry
therefore rich.

If the bull's a beast of few words
and thus absent even when around,
the cow unable to write her novel or to properly self-actualize,
then it's a Feminist poem and that's no joke.

If the poem willfully but playfully confuses "cow"
with the Dow (you know how slippery words are!),
it's of the Language variety.
The Dow's always off to market jiggedy-jig,
dropping well-meaning meaning like cow pies stepped in,
shoes amuck as Ben Bernanke's bull.
Don't even check your balance.

If there's Derrida ladled in, the milk's deconstructed
hence curdled.

If the cow and bull huddle in twilight
hard by the dark-stone-earth-blood-mother-dark-stone-shadow,
it's a Deep Image poem
but most of them end up butchered.

If the bull China-shop drops country fences
and pilfers others' grass
to secure our freedom as well as theirs,
it's a Surrealist poem
or a *New York Times* op-ed on the Bush presidency.

If the cow kisses and tells then aborts,
it's a Confessional poem.
Ditto the bull's drug habit.

If the cow seems just a cow, the fence wooden,
that bull mere lust on four hooves—beware.
Never does a poem unfold the blanket of its white lie
without wine in a picnic basket, without cheese
and the guitar whose notes your hand strums.

Apple Blossoms at Petal-Fall with Li Po

That a cardinal's bright dart alights upon the branch
means *Non cogito, ergo sum*—
I don't think, therefore I am.

But that's not Mandarin!
Still the tree's petal-fall dusts us angelic,
our arms feathered wings.

A fool's errand, this search for meaning,
metaphor the bed we lie and awaken in.
Hey there, get off our cloud!

In this we grow lonely though not alone,
the way my Cortland shimmers
in a cloud of her own making.

I know what I said. I said *her*.
You'd like to know what I make
of her secret, also ours.

Try this: forget the fate we'll share,
warm from the oven of our unmaking,
soon these limbs winter bare.

Just don't, let's say,
our arms petaled feathers.
This once: *Don't think*.

April Ode to a Petunia That Outlived Winter

You are beautiful and lucky.
I hate you.
We loathe the one in whom our flaws are made right.
What are you but wordless musical flesh?

You can't care the Afghani girl's lost her legs
to our nation's (mis)guided missile,
or even that my dog piddles upon your roots.
On this you thrive.

You are lucky. You are beautiful.
I hate how I care though still do nothing
about the good boy plunked dead
outside his dead school.

A life is made as much by its refusals
as by yes. On this I thrive.
You are beautiful and I am lucky
to be lucky enough. In this we are kin.

You should not be here, nor *be* at all.
What are you, wind-spilled dross,
seed the vole stole away and forgot?
What beneath snow but patience?

What are we but mistake made lovely
by mistake?
Tell me *where do we come from,*
what are we, where are we going?

Brother, our flesh is flower
doomed to flower.

THE GOOD DOG'S VALENTINE CENTO

If ever two were one, then surely we.
We real cool.
In a holy place with a god I walked
when two roads diverged in a yellow wood
and I chased the deer less young.
Let us go then, you and I,
while pheasants are nesting and the coyotes few,
while the narrow fellow in the grass stitches little blue stem ahead of us.
There is a parrot imitating spring,
there is a singer no one has heard.
Do I contradict myself?
I have had to learn the simplest things last,
thus my begging eyes——
and that has made all the difference.
Once upon a midnight dreary
I saw the best fetchers of my generation
destroyed by lameness, starving toothless.
I've known rivers.
Make me, oh Lord, thy swimming wheel,
the soul as buoyant as a tossed stick.
I wake to sleep, and take my waking slow
when the postman knocks for you.
Such tink and tank and tunk-a-tunk-tunk
just off the highway to Rochester, Minnesota,
for after lunch I snore like a bullhorn.
Your thighs are appletrees
by which I mean a compliment.
Very well, then, I contradict myself.
I contain multitudes
of lick and bark, of sunrise walk and moonful howl.
All things within this fading world hath end
upon the short leash hung beside the door.

I, too, dislike it.
From my mother's sleep I fell into
our house and yard, the neighbors' fence I could not burrow under,
garbage the poem of our time.
I've known bed and bowl and occasional bath,
swimming upstream until its current pushed me back to your feet.
So much depends upon my nap's red wheelbarrow,
glazed with sunlight beside the white curtains.

6 Chair's Lift Line, Breckenridge

- An apple's the teacher's pet of fruits, always begging *me, me, me*.
- First in line's blushed Yellow Delicious or tinged Honey Crisp.
- It's the blonde who looks your way with her eyes' curtains closed.
- Another churning's the galactic hooha Lady Gaga snowfalls money of.
- Snow's desire in white disguise as is Lady who prefers the banana.
- An Italian couple's busy ignoring *Please Alternate* because it's language.
- When a patroller bids the kumquats *Stop*, they in their tracks do.
- The lifework of the orange is to be juicy and unrhymable.
- An orange storage shed marked High Voltage approximates both.
- Peeling an orange resembles undressing a woman only in rudimentary yearning.
- It's pears breasts resemble layered in down like grounded birds.
- The kiwi resembles a green eye symmetry gives us two of but not the seed complete.
- When fate proffers lemons, imagine women wedged in a maze awaiting your ride.
- That's a mirage, as is Mt. Helen's holding hands with Father Dyer Peak.
- Grapes give us wine which is thank you to please as sky is to ground.
- In this light the Ten Mile Range happily tongues a tangerine horizon.
- Snow, says Li Po, is besotted gods' *grabbing a cloud and grinding it into white dust*.
- At least that's what translator David Hinton says Li Po says in stitched lines.
- The poem's first word faces forward, the rest a helmeted back of head sliding away.
- We're bound for chairs lifting each by each above the white eternal.
- Be of good cheer, my friends, for the ride, signs say, lasts a mere ten minutes.

Upon Seeing, in Shadow, a Red Tail Hawk Plunder the Songbird's Nest

It's not the poetic fact of sun and shade,
nor the hatchlings' peeping, bobbing heads,

commotion of motion, eye, and light.
Not even the raptor's rapt intent.

It's the seeing in shadow
as if from Plato's cave, though

my seeing's a jumble of fact
and artful act—

the way of painting and landscape's primal dance,
of dance itself— which is space

and time given the body
of chance, this vivid god.

It's chance we greet with flinch
or sigh, kneeling as with any punch

or blessing, something on wing
from sky so unforgiving

I saw not hawk but hawk's shadow
swoop above the ground I mow.

Saw then the pillaged fledglings,
shadow nest of featherless wings,

these who'll fly
but once in the Red Tail's belly.

ANTIPHON FOR LES PAUL

Without Les Paul, we'd not have rock and roll
as we know it.
—Terry Stewart / Rock and Roll Hall of Fame

We awaited you, our instrument of ascension,
after the Chattanooga choo-choo toot-tooted daddy home,
after mom crooned her sugared we've-never-lost-a-war solo.

We awaited your invention's inventing us,
dreamscaping our yet unstaired stairway to heaven,
youth as stillborn as Sinatra sung by Sinatra Jr.,
awaiting the radio's Ray-O-Vac she loves you
ringing its yeah yeah yeah imperative within us.

   Audacity is wisdom's uncultured pearl.

We awaited our ticket to ride khakis and Madras
button-downs, bobby socks innocence yet to goose-bump
our brown-eyed girl, wallflowers shoulder to shoulder,
awaiting dizzy miss Lizzy's penciled drumbeat—
our leaded voices as silent as the white room.

We awaited you instead of the new boss same as
the old boss, you of buzz and microphone drone,
you of immigrant songs soon to shock
The Man's big band ashtray of tenured butts,
our chain-smoked century's chain of fools.

   Wisdom is audacity's cultured pearl.

M-m-my generation waited unamplified—

necklaced by wars—vowing we'll not get fooled again
on Christmas morn, eggnogged and groggy,
while the Great Folk Song Revival offered up
the tambourine man's spangled acoustic.

Then *The Log* arrived, your 4" by 4" wooden chunk
strung with steel strings, pickups, and that sound.
Its anthemic growl birthed us from one mother into another
from whom we emerged electric motherfuckers:
squealing pineal wail adolescent angst christ devil.

    Purity's a measure of what's not there.

It's your church hymns we hum, refusing to floss
or fund an IRA. It's your dogma fuse credo vatic path:
lilting big daddy death's never pulling the plug on us.

SON ROOM

Freud's Swiss Army Knife opened the spectral lid
of the unconscious
with no less awe than we this door.

Here myth's kite snagged adolescent power lines,
down that string the primal electric flicking his body's switches.
This boy, his own executioner.

We of the bad back
walk among the ruins of what we've made
now unmade into his own.

Once his tractor plowed this pocked hardwood
among blocks and Matchbox wrecks,
amid scuffed baseballs and Lego shambles.

Now the vestigial and iconic lie,
awaiting the lie.
Impatience rules where clocks tick not tock enough.

Waiting marks the province of old folks,
mewling how a son's age ages them.
The room's text message to grownups: *gro up!*

This, the young man's last lost domain,
facile castle where everything's resolved
by guns and balls.

NIGHT VISIT TO THE RECYCLING CENTER, A THREE-ALBUM BOX SET

I.

The door's plastic whoosh time-machined me
back to pinched-open album wrappers, back to
vinyl offered the godly turntable's incense-rites,
liner notes and artsy photo shadow revelations
where a guy, if so inclined, rolled doobies.
Tick tock weeks went up in smoke. What's
cliché but metaphor first apt, thereafter not?

2.

The sign's recycling arrows curled into each other
the way we danced but couldn't stop that war,
a needle dropped into the groove and then
into us, going in circles our usual human state.
Vinyl once was oil and before that ferns upon
a hillside. Turns out dead stuff fuels the living.
Language, claims Emerson, is fossilized metaphor.

3.

In half-light a conveyor looped into itself
as I did shaving my wheelchaired father,
Count Basie chasing his tail upon the Victrola's
spinning platter. My hand scratched its shaky
tune across his chin, notes hummed off key
as will my son for me. So close his breath fogged
my glasses. Now so far I've lost him in cloud.

Parable of the Sentence

Music's the lyric's Master Card, jauntily
　derailing meaning's choo choo train,
　　the sentence our lost locomotive.

Hold onto your wallet when the poet lilts
　of his "blonde moon," beauty vapid but efficient
　　in the fashion of *Mademoiselle*, and napalm.

Back in the day a poem fed upon caboose
　as much as engine, all that chugging
　　beginning and ending a period with one.

Subect we *verb* waited for coupling's
　object syntax, our Penn Central,
　　the B & O, the Reading line linked,

certain what was coming would end
　with kerchiefed men waving from a window,
　　the swaying red lantern's satisfaction.

Everywhere great arms lifted, steeled wheels
　clank-clunked, and what one knew moved
　　inexorably distant but still on track. Period.

Everything on track. AIG, Standard Oil, GM,
　dogs napping in slant sun. Everything,
　　the baby in her bathwater, on track.

Our President not yet explaining how
　the known unknowns won't get you
　　but the unknown unknowns will.

Tracks on everything, even the moon,
   certainty as shiny as the Shah's gold bed.
      Collateral and *damage* not yet wed.

Everything on track. Isn't it pretty?
   All things verbed, the sentence so trusted
   signs point us the way home.

ARS POETICA @ 59

> *The boring, yapping schools*
> *of beat and slick.*
> *They make me sick.*
> *—James Wright*
> *(unpublished, circa 1961)*

I think poems beginning *I think* need not
be dead on arrival, cleaving the art of thought
from the earthly body poetry also shares.
Who says a poem can't both sing *and* mean?
Friends, the world's got to get in there
but often doesn't, so our poe-biz scene's
unchanged since Emerson's bemoaned schism
sliced the party of *memory* from that of *hope*.
Poetry's split personality meant dualism
parted the poets of *highbrow* and *low*, a trope

for the indelicate division of *paleface*
from *redskin*, purging of the *mythic*
from the *Adamic*, and Lowell's tracing
a line between *cooked* and *un-*. That rhetoric
proved as pitiless as our current fetish
for feckless squabbles pitting *workshop* verse
against ethnopoetics most profs don't relish.
Art's red-faced handslap we've rehearsed
through centuries of crackpot aesthetic duels
whose cheeky winner is always the rules.

What smacks new since too-polite Wright
dared to scribble his bilious mini-*ars* then hid it?
Well, we learned the merits of Confessional chat

exceed that of scuba as mode of descent,
meaning Wright's "Can you hear me?"
mimics Hamlet's "To be or not to be."
Because the world's got to get in there
but often doesn't, we learned his yapping bores
still bedevil our verse, supplicants on knee before
idols sculpted of dryer vent fuzz or rotted pear.

On one side reside the weary but proud
envoys of tweed, nose hairs raised to the clouds.
On the other aisle abide the doyens of howl
and yawp, our rumpled purveyors of soul.
Where, dear reader, stand you? Which camp
would likely suffer me? Whose hand will stamp
our literary passports if poetry's Snuggie morphs
from underpants yank to that commercial's goofy
blanket-monk, shutting out cold as well as our planet?
When the world doesn't get in there, the poet's

a mindless one-man-band tone deaf to our
timpani symphony—dark notes of a bloody hour.
It's true the *ars poetica* twisted from fiery tract
to personal ad: "SWM seeking long walks,
bookstore snuggling, and the Academy's handshake."
At best it spews cracked hendecasyllabics.
Even our rebel Language clan's stumbling,
mumbling how *pizza* and *piazza* nearly read the same,
wordplay of more consequence than bumbling
Joni Mitchell's refusing Woodstock's flame

for Dick Cavett Show's yellow paycheck.
It's true our acts are words but not. Think
how history might not have blinked
had Joni sung amid the mud instead of penning

"Woodstock" about a place she'd never been.
My first *ars* sillily rhymed Joni with "phony" then
justly thanked her for making a wrong
right by getting the world in there—this, my reply
to Mrs. Sweet's cloying classroom ploy
to silence what meager protest songs

I'd muster. "Dear, Dear Boy," she oozed,
"why write poems?" Say their sinews
carry the news we've not yet made word.
Say ink like blood thrums its blues
upon the stringed instrument of compassion.
Say those bombers Joni so loathed
turned "into butterflies above our nation"
even if you didn't drop acid, though four-dead-
in-Ohio made politicians freak as if they had.
Say poetry like science has nosed

its share of the elevated answers
if not a cure for ovarian cancer.
Say poems welcome the world's big show,
philosophers and strippers and politicos,
the homeless bloom of daffodils in snow,
larder of our earthly carnival. Say poems fly
inside us as if orbiting the globe on high.
Say this, friends—poetry's the human Space Station
where schoolkids launch Painted Lady chrysalisae
morphing to butterflies above our bankrupt nation.

2

Ballad of Trouvadore

In route to Santiago, Cuba, in 1841, the Spanish brigantine
slave ship Trouvadore ran aground on Breezy Point in the Turks
and Caicos Islands, then a British colony. Trouvadore, likely
misspelling of Troubadour, Spanish for "wandering minstrel,"
carried a crew of 20 and a cargo of 193 West African slaves.

I. The Slaver

February 1ˢᵗ / West Africa

I do midnight work, the thing done when no one's looking.
When gods sleep slump-shouldered, weary
of hungry prayers, tired of mouths always empty never shut.
Loan me creation's fist and I'd shut them up.

February 3rd

At home my father asked, "Why do this work?"
Better than dragging a plough through dust
from which we came and to which we . . . ,
our little cloud trailing a curse the room forgets
once the door's slammed shut.
Bang, a harrow shoulders the dust's tiny doors.
Bang, of made and unmade.
At least I ride the seas.
The ocean's a rolling ranch, this ship my bucking horse,
and these I shush from place to place my black cattle.
There's coins' clack, a belly full, the beard trimmed.
My work is to herd, for which I'm paid.
Their work is to slave.

February 5th

Prayer's begging I lack stomach for,
the knees creaking please. Pity this:
I wanted black bread for my table, a blanket for my bed,
and please Angelina Tomasia nestled please
beneath its holey wool pleasing me.
O Most Holy, O Most Powerful, O Most Mighty—
Shit, I won't beg.

Even gods sicken of too much praise
as men spew of too much wine—
the head hammered, tongue pinched in great tongs
your words can't wriggle free of, gut punched.
What had gone so sweet down the throat
now spouts bitter back out,
a gaggle of devils siphoning its sugars.
Not even a god who turned water into wine
makes prayer of vomit.

February 11th

We scouted thatched huts, sorted and counted.
We watched the stream they wade in,
water jugs balanced upon women's heads.
We watched who lugs and carries, who tends their young.
We watched the muscled men and boys, sifted
their old aside. We watched and counted those
we'll shoot to make our point.
We watched because gods did not,
our midnight work to watch and tally:
89 men, 26 women, 39 boys, 11 girls, 3 infants.

February 13th

Easy, boys, I sang to my mates. Smile as does
your musket. Smile so smile befits you both,
their trust your powder and plug. *Easy does it, boys.*

February 15th

Rustlers unfettered, we drove our herd to beach,
the shufflers neck-shackled with chain.
They glistened the black and blue of bruise,
of sun hanged on string from the heavenly fist.
While gods slept, their vacant eyes closed.
While ticking ticked off their hellish clock.
While I ogled the women to see they'd all
the parts I'll get my hands on, my cock in.
One licorice bitch with eyes of stone
flung them at me, as if her look would knock
my head aright. She nursed an infant, cradled
the ebony, hummed a thing akin to song.
Sunlit breast milk pearled, her ornament and oath.

February 19th

Today the sea bent like grass wind moved through,
this ship my bay mare at canter shoulder deep.
No god's hand held us up—afloat, akilter, alive.
We rode the belly of a slumbering beast.
Each breath's rising, each exhale's sudden bottom
begged of faith and fear. I've neither.

February 25th

So cloudless this morn I opened slotted louvers
to air our cargo. If not for their singing,

I'd have forgotten *this* hell beneath my buoyant feet
as I've discarded the other. Forgotten the rank
and rot and shit they puddled in. Forgotten
their word for water, those hands upraised.
One mate, a Portuguese of Sào Tomé, enflamed
by their pleas as gods get hot with ours,
pissed on those below: "Drink that!"
as if his spritz would douse his fire and theirs.

March 2nd

At sunset the eyeglass spied a vessel, Brits
who'd free our payload. Captain Velasea veered
hard toward squall, losing that ship in night storm.
I shut the cargo slots to keep rain out and us afloat.
Through each slit I met their faces, swallowed
in the ship's belly riding a wave's belly. Their eyes—
or the salt spray—bid me do the job with mine shut.

March 3rd

Trouvadore creaked on prayer's knees, her timbers
betraying the zeal of the recently converted.
Could she have listened, I'd have told what little
profit comes of that. Of want prayer's made, as is sex.
Of want the ship heaved, of want she shuddered,
want feeding want until the deed was done,
fate's seed settled in her, grounded in shallows.
Captain, wagering tide will lift us off reef,
ordered us ashore with cargo in rope tow.
My dry powder downed the first slave who ran
for the bush. His blood stilled the rest.

March 4th / Breezy Point, East Caicos Island

First light upturned the night sky, the beach
a constellation of black stars on white sand,
their faces charting our lost course, aflame.
When locals blundered up, Captain gifted his silver
for a ship. In thanks, those bastards delivered
Lt. Fitzgerald's lockstep Brits, muskets cocked.

March 5th

Swaggering, they marched us to the island's courthouse,
we the prodded cattle, chattel in our own chains.
Our midnight work, thing done when no one's looking,
unmasked in noon sun. Never had I noticed
the clack of chains so like the clink of coins.
Never had I seen a woman with eyes of stone
blaze with light, the bleary gods awakened in hers.

March 30th / Santiago, Cuba

Landfall, home but not.
Next time, I'll not get caught.

II. The Woman with Eyes of

There was not and the forsaken who

•

There was malice in words as water in tears of

•

There was song, the pitcher filled with

•

There was not and the forsaken who now

•

There was the slaver eying me but blind to

•

There was breath and the taken from

•

There was the face of day, the bowl of sky I did not

•

There was a child in my arms and the man in chains who

•

There was my bridal dance in hand with

•

There was rain to drink but the sea not to

•

There was not and the forsaken who now walk

•

There was home, this island but neither of

•

There was earth and sky, the emptiness between

•

There was under and the flesh upon which

•

There was hair upon his devil's face and the hidden in

•

There was skin and the loathing of

•

There was not and the forsaken who now walk free.

Opening the Washing Machine's New Burstless Hoses, Made in China, I Think of

whose hands wrapped these string ties, red stripe hot,
 you whose twist arcs a bend as perfect and tireless

 as any machine's, whose tired human bloom blooms
perfect as sunlight from a lone high window cupping your up-

turned face as does Lu Chen when you lie wrapped around
 the day's labor bedded down with goose down, the two of

 you perfectly tired, chill filling the space your bellies belly to
belly can't touch,

you whose hands wrapped these string ties, blue stripe cold,
 whose twist arcs as perfectly tireless as machine lips'

 kiss-kiss-release, its chill cheek upon yours tethered to this
hose wrapped in my unfolded hands, the unmade prayer work

answers for me on knee among the laundry, you bent penitent
 to the hour's task, whose measure measures not soul

 but absence we peer through, this umbilical linking us eye
to blind eye.

Blind Voyeur

To verify images kills them . . . it is always more
enriching to imagine *than to* experience.
—Gaston Bachelard

This isn't Sophoclean in the fashion of putting
one's eyes out. His notion is nearer the mind's *eye*—
singular—as if it's the Cyclops that still sees
even after a spear's tossed through it.
Post-supper he's backseat king of the wife's
unwashed Ford, dish-drying Ray Charles windows
he can't see out or in, putt-putting the neighborhood
not tragic if Mrs. Brown's imagined alight with blush,
her foot-worn carpet and cat-scratched couch,
leek and bloody sausage spicing no matter what
Mozart or Motown, what Bach of hip-hop thumps
her upswept bouffant, the hair gray with winter.
Kitty-corner the Joneses packed off to Iraq
and one come legless home, Dick's seasick mother
whisked off the immigrant boat with hope's luggage
later pillaged while poppa looked for work.
There's the pickup truck chucked on concrete blocks,
rusted flagpole bent at the waist thus bowing
to the cast-off loveseat teenagers neck upon,
ankles yanked shut when mom stomps up to cook.
How it molders the ramshackle porch and can't be sat
in August when fleas beset it, thirsty for thigh blood.
How Jackson's black lawn jockey lifts its lantern,
footman of an unenlightened past that will not pass,
Uncle Saul's death-bed mattress atilt against
an orange storage shed. How it signifies sleep
the sleeper sees not out of but in to, as is the manner

of his eyes open even when closed. Each evening
imagination's white lie spills from him like his yard's
toppled wheelbarrow now lush with petunias,
illusion of catastrophe gone artfully to blossom.

Sputnik Summer

You could borrow a guy's mitt but not his cap,
    that summer
sun's cauldron boiled the bowl of sugar maples
    arcing
the outfield fence and pitching down the ditch
    where old men
tipped paper-sacked Mogen David and no ball
    ever came
back. Even nuns' yardsticks hadn't saved us,
    so we'd *screw-you*
the bastard drunks then run because we could.

Fearing priests more than Commies, I didn't pray
    for world peace
when Jigger's fastball Sputniked off my bat
    then rocketed
the road where ambulances birthed stretchered
    progeny,
nor when the ball reentered earth's atmosphere,
    dropped ballistic
through animal cracker clouds then crash-glass-
    landed
upon the hospital window's dirt-scrawled steppe.

No one yet fretted what the inscrutable *Ruskies*
    were up to
when sirens wailed Tuesday noon. Feet etched
    a diamond
upon the sparse grass, its bases can lids tossed
    in dust,
home a ketchupy mess black ants relinquished
    with one stitch

across the batter's sockless ankles. The limits
       of chain link
and our power kept a score we knew by heart.

If the Battle of Waterloo was won upon Eton's
       playing fields,
Vietnam was lost amid our strike-outs and dropped
       pop ups.
So first we heard then saw them, their unstoppered
       voices
pouring out the window-mouth's broken *Oh*:
       the polio ward's
stick kids clutching crutches, metal-braced in place,
       the ketchup-haired boy
back-flat within his iron lung's antiseptic dystopia.

They hooted their clattering metal, rubber-tipped cheer,
       our audience
announcing they were not fit for pity. We did not offer
       a sweaty cap
salute. We did not curse crooked fate's twisted limbs,
       nor wipe
the febrile brow of luck with the cotton of our prayer.
       I stood
stiff as they, moved but unmoving, raising the silly
       stars and stripes
of ignorance up the pole of my able body.

FORGIVEN

Because it rained because the night

    a physics teacher plied you

with booze and smoke,

      because his blue-steel pistol,

you undressed your living room

      piece by peace

    upon the wet front lawn.

Because even night zippered

    down his calloused hands,

you shouldered the sofa upon the grass,

      hauled those chairs one two three,

    because a mirror's drenched jewel.

Because water ran as you did,

    zigzagging his off-shot,

    because he missed,

      you made home there,

the shower showering you.

Because the Big Bang banged,

the universal furniture blown apart,

because its genesis of sex and loneliness,

you forgave yourself yourself.

ON THE MERITS OF GRADUATE EDUCATION

When first he shoveled up the courage to intone on the phenomeno-logical implications of caves in Shelley's work, the wire-rimmed blonde barked at him, *ruff, ruff.* This one, he shuddered, knows her Feminist Theory, bracing for the onslaught. But nothing. The seminar shifted their wooden rears in pine chairs, the professor nodded knowingly, and silence stoked the furnace of his paranoia—ah, to be a fool before his Ivied peers! His ears wilted and fell petaled upon this tabled disgrace.

When later he gave forth on negative capability, she *ruff-ruffed* so uncontrollably it muzzled him, tongue-tied and abashed, in the cross hairs of academic exchange. While the professor built a tower of Romantic cant, students knelt in awed abeyance. Only her guttural *ruff, ruff* could lay siege to this turret—the blonde's mantra rising to *jerk face jack off tallywacker* catapulted with such force over the flaming gates he cringed as *bullshit* shot from her half-cocked mouth as if from a crossbow whose trigger she didn't finger.

When last her body twitched as if a fish on dock, late afternoon light spilling the twist of Tourette's, it came to him how Samuel Johnson suffered its tic and affliction before there was name or even definition in *A Dictionary of the English Language.* Her sudden tears doused the flames of his paranoia. So he's not the bumbling fool, he's not the class idiot. *She is,* he gloated. *She is,* his fist pounded the fine pine table, as the room and its cushionless chairs spun a giddy axis around him, around him.

Special Olympics

Bobby birthed a blue room laboring to say what love's

    *   *

labor brought forth. Rebecca lay upon a bed twisted

    *   *

and absolved, learned to crawl by three, rode the short bus.

    *   *

Enrico survived the glinting knife-and-fork stares of

    *   *

restaurant-goers and the checkout's sucker condescension

    *   *

disguised as lollypop. Timmy's snickering schoolmates

    *   *

feared the strange as they feared themselves unknowable.

    *   *

Maddox ran a sideways race and swam the sunken lap

    *   *

for ribbons "your contribution generously provides."

         *   *

Wendi mounted a podium to savor the August embrace

         *   *

of parents, proud and remade. My Oliver clattered a giddy

         *   *

bike down roads he named by riding, child of the akilter,

         *

perfectly imperfect.

Parable of the Narrative

Chapter 1

O'Hare's planes sat shrink-wrapped with ice,
so nothing's humping or getting humped on Hump Day.
Desperate strangers, stranded,

we three assumed the rented life
of Hertz' dirty-diaper Chevy,
whose headlamps once shimmied down

my hometown's unionized assembly line
before NAFTA dominoed my second Viet Nam—
the body count bloody economic.

Chapter 2

At lunch the driver's flummoxed ex texted
to ask about the buried power line.
Hers was a question of location not guilt.

Back then they fashioned it home addition,
though the result was long division.
Without power there's no TV, or sex.

Even the holy Dalai Lama, not wholly
without desire, tires of unanswered prayer,
yearning as electric as the ex's "huny cum ovr."

Chapter 3

Cue segue's violins. He's watching her sleep,
undraped moonlight cheap but still not free.
Then he's dodging Taliban RPGs.

Back home she rode his techie neighbor,
computer guru of buzz,
huffing aerosol for the snake-hiss lift

she titled "Walking on Sunlight,"
her drug-spun Harlequin.
Unanswered prayer's redundant in time of war.

Chapter 4

Across pot-holed-prairie,
our afternoon of Arabian nights,
he spun for us Kandahar's blustery dusk,

then moonlit streets of the fallen
who might be said to sleep
but no they're dead—

a story that bored the backseat professor
preferring post-Colonialism
to explosion.

Chapter 5

Narratologists suggest each story auditions endings.
Todorov, the wild one, claims all stories spill
from the belly of a single sentence, mother

of the waters proper proper-nouns steep in.
What happens to happen births from small choice.
Say this: The Evil (*king, dragon, terrorist*)

threatens innocent (*peasant, damsel, American Way of Life*)
until the awful conflagration when divine order
is momentarily (*restored, defeated*). Big story.

Chapter 6

South of Hopewell, metaphor and gas stop,
sunset through pink sunglasses, the end his ending.
Once his Humvee growled, iPod jamming AC/DC

snaking daybreak's patrol, poppies strung with mist
and wires. Gently, his blade milked the bloom.
Each tear bled tears, Christ's or Mohammed's.

Blood resin seeped from wounds it heals—heals
if smoked. *THE END* means it's over but not.
Kaboom. Narrative's a drug.

To Illinois's Gold Star Mothers, Who Lost a Child to War

By 1936 Congressional Resolution, the last Sunday
in September is designated as Gold Star Mother's Day.

You know these names as more than polished stone,
   more even than ink on white parchment.
     You know the child awash with chocolate,
       the lanky one whose knees no jeans could hold.

     You know the face you've framed upon the wall,
   those eyes as lush as June lilies, that hair
as wild as the river after spring rains.

You know the one who shouldered burdens
   asked of him. You know *sacrifice* because
     she gave you the word whole, in act and deed
       of hour upon lonesome hour. You know these,

     and shall not forget the way you learned by heart
   what it means to birth and to give away. Mothers
know how mothers greet sun's yellow umbrella

unfolding from Kankakee to Cairo,
   Watseka to Buffalo Grove to Rock Island—
     arcing from there to Tokyo and Seoul,
       Berlin to London, Kabul to Baghdad.

     You know why sunrise portends sunset, realm
   of the asked and the given. Your nation's born of
more than stone, more than ink on white parchment.

In the Interest of Brevity, Let's Begin at the End

.   Now that's done, so let's get on with life,
this distillation of collage as refined as sugar
but often bittersweet. Its hodgepodge precedes
the period, a sign saying *stay tuned* the way
one does after commercials or a funeral.
If lucky, one tastes sugar because a pattern's set.
But art loves eyes where the hair should be,
surprise sputtering hiccups spelled hiccoughs
also spelled fate—which in life becomes
a wife's portrait installed in the living room
with all the attendant hoo-ha, she surviving
cancer but not my lame *Lovely without Hair*,
sighing, "Those aren't my eyes."

∞

Snowy days a red-bellied woodpecker visits her,
head redder than his misnomer belly tight against
the tree, bark flying spent shells from the rifle
of his beak. Viewed from the living room window
they're a community not unlike the Bauhaus
old Gropius envisioned as populist "eclecticism,"
his notion so *electric* my confusing the two bristles
serendipitous. Morning's ironic rhyme ice is AKA
hoar frost—the former poetic, the latter faintly whorish
in the manner black lace complicates its virginal twin.
Now it filigrees each branch with Irish lace,
art the bird and she have made alive together,
as are we.

∞

Mona Lisa was pregnant when Leonardo
painted her, no wonder the coy tumescent smile,
the great master plugged-in to beginnings.
Electricity moves one's hand in such moments,
its spark inventing the highway median reflector
and the AK-47 though hopefully something
more life-sustaining, say, the medical catheter
or Moholy-Nagy's "Light Space Modulator"
fusing luminosity, color, and movement—as did
Muhammad Ali in the ring and out. Killing is said
to be Cain's invention, a beginning composed wholly
of endings. Refusing war's rifle and thereby Cain,
Ali made art of a floating butterfly, the stinging bee.

∞

Electricity moves one's hand in such moments,
rhyming punch drunk before a portrait I can't
remember painting. What the Bauhaus meant by
awakening "the personal life inherent in the form"
resides in a woman's breast rescued from cancer
because some soulful geek created the catheter,
collage of science and art. In Breckenridge
she of lost hair begins each game with the anthem.
The Summit High Tigers clack their hockey sticks
upon the home ice when she sings "free."
In that instant everything's electric possibility
slippery beneath the feet, even irony
checked at the door with one's coat and hat.

3

THE AFTERLIFE

As a priest marries the Church   so I wed work.
The union's tin ring, a fin per   week and nothing
down. Trouble was, everything   *was* down:
the line, my pay, the pickup's   windows in rain.
The blonde in shipping couldn't   keep lunch down
or her pants up. Damp her sloppy   tears, damp the shirt's
pits, damp the Chevy's back seat   where rum and Cokes
broke the ice. Her lesson? Never   operate heavy machinery
with lips and zipper. My hands   made feral love
to chill metal, worksong of parts   I'd never see whole
so boys, smoke 'em if you've got   'em. Smokes made ash,
the dust from which ye came and   to dust ye shall.
Dust upon the riven garden. Dust   at neck and sleeves
of my black pocket tee, dust etching   each night's second
shower, my chest the archaic torso   of unionized Apollo.
School's velvet Rilke counseled me,   "You must change your life."
Though I wished his face so near   I could punch it,
language I understood I could not   understand
changed me for the price of student   loans and Latin.
I'm living the afterlife—these hands   uncalloused,
tweed houndstoothed, my dust become   the stuff of
stacked books. I'm living the afterlife   for those who cut
then polish, lug and heave, who stack   mortise and miter
swing shift. They don't need my guilt   or your pity.
Change is what's fisted back from our   broken dollar.
Change is stashed by the backdoor in a   cracked Ball jar.

TODAY I WAS HAPPY, SO I MADE THIS POEM

Death's not the most depressing thing to write about
but writing about it is.
Incessantly fretting you'll hammer a thumb
trebles the hurt of actually doing it.
Kids doing Jumping Jacks are named Jack
only when they are.
The Lincoln penny costs more to make than it's worth.
Adopting the cop dog shot in a drug bust
gives his paws pause.
The nuthatch walks head-down down a tree trunk
but not walking back up.
Jumping's what they're doing only in the figurative sense.
Your bedroom dresser doesn't actually dress you,
but cherry's a nice accent.
Walking head-down back up the trunk would be backing up.
Death depends upon what the definition of *is* is.
Montezuma's Blue Cloud Coffeehouse sold my books
if sold means free stains.
Each year thirteen billion pennies are minted
but not of mint.
Copper's what the bad guys grunted when busted.
The definition of *is* preceded that of *was*.
Was necessitated Samuel Johnson's inventing the dictionary.
Johnson invented the white-fro mullet for Reynolds's portrait.
Incessantly fretting you'll hammer a thumb
trebles the hurt of actually doing it.
I said that before really means you're not listening.
The drug dog's licking his yard a peace sign of yellowed grass.
Detritus has *us* in it, and that's no joke.
There's no *Free Lunch* now that the magazine's gone under.
Newsweek's yearly list of who's gone under is less depressing
when read upside down.

Not a single title in *The Norton Anthology of Postmodern Poetry*
begins with "death."
Andrew Marvell's writing about dying made his coy mistress horny.
Nothing begins with death.
The title "Today I Was Happy, So I Made This Poem"
was lifted from James Wright with permission of the nuthatch
heading down head-down.
The rescued dog named
"I Heard a Fly Buzz Do Not Go Gentle into That Good Night"
is called Happy.

CARDINAL NUMBERS:
SEQUENCE IN WHICH NO ONE DIES

> *During mating season, the male cardinal may become so transfixed by its window-glass reflection, it will court, or tirelessly attack, this likeness.*
> —The Audubon Book of Birds

I

Morning's Narcissus,
a cardinal thrusts himself against the glass, against himself,
thump, then thump,
his body and its reflection nearly one but for the looking glass
he can't pass by
nor pass through.
Pretty *birdie, birdie, birdie* he flutes at first light,
posing, cocksure,
so in love he'll thrash feather dust and crack beak,
song his lament.

3

No one I know is dying.
For once I'm whole, divisible by one and myself.
Meaning I'm prime, cardinal—the antithesis of antithesis.
I am the apple and its wind-blown shadow.
I am rain cloud and solitary drop.
I am the daisy and wet dirt, what's falling and the space between.
I am rain and the match that sputters but not
out.

5

When workmen shouldered our new carpet in,
their tune was AC/DC, Slayer, and armpit sweat.
Sleeveless then, the men, their grunts and heaves,
knives as sharp as pirates' curses
and their curses, too,
even a thin one with eye patch and tattoo envied for lyrical abandon:
parrot head upon his shoulder as red as
the cardinal in love with love.

7

No flushing chemo,
no blessing the hospice bed,
no shoveling a drawer for the policy
or that photo of mama on a cruise that was her next
to last.
For once no one's riding the night train to Memphis
where all the Egyptian gods, like Elvis,
grace big houses.

11

What, maybe a week's scent,
new carpet bouquet we savored when we didn't know toxic?
Then spaghetti's spilled, pizza and ice cream,
some sloshed concoction a kid grows his lime green moustache from.

13

After his last rites, my uncle shooed everyone from the room
in favor of his Western's last chapter, saying,
"Now, to get Joe Cardinal out of the fix I'm in."

17

After their tan Dodge van smoke break,
the tool-boxed flask of Jack,
it's quick back at it—
so, too, the window-whacking bird,
his self-love unrequited.
Drunk on berries, beak and tuft, his wings serrated knives,
the cardinal thumped glass in time with
Slayer's sledgehammer drummer,
the too-thin carpet men halting in mid-seam, feathered
by his abandon.

19

Do not wither thinner, boys,
for a shadow no longer casts one.

23

The first daisy has opened its rain-clean face
and bees the last apple blossom,
a wink against the night.
No one I love is dying any faster than our usual
spiral.
Not even the absurd redbird who loves himself
as a match loves flame.

Endnotes to the Poem "Touch" Lost with a Crashed Hard Drive

[1] It's true T. S. Eliot's father warned "She'll put your eye out,"
hers "He'll ring your bell,"
though their intent was figurative not literal.

[2] Touch-me-not alludes both to jewelweed blooms
and the garden's squirting cucumber.

[3] Touchwood refers to stuff that ignites:
thus tinder is to fire
as tender is the touchstone of touch.

[4] Uncorking was Eliot's metaphor for the perils of desire.

[5] The demotic French translates, unbuttoned,
"Is that champagne chilled?"

[6] Touchhole delineates the cannon vent through which its charge is lit.

[7] The phrase "is now and ever shall be, world without end, amen"
is stolen from prayer, therefore doubling the sin.

[8] The couple's coupling in church quadruples their sin,
evoking both cannon-fire and the cops.

[9] Lord Byron, Romantic chore boy,
kicked the bucket while love-mopping the Greek Isles.
His heart is buried there, the body shipped home in a liquor barrel.

[10] Touch descends from Middle English *touchen*, Old French *touchier*,
from Old Latin *toccare*, "to knock or strike like a bell."
Lovers thus ring with peals of pleasure.

[11] The cathedral of the body calls it worship.

SUNRISE, SNOWFALL, TWO CROWS AMONG LODGEPOLE PINES

I am unworthy of this gift,

    let's agree on that,

  this mercury of desire

I've tunneled for

    only to discover on wing.

  This breeze add to the list,

this painting not brushed

    of oils on cloth. This snow

  giving body one sees only

in the arms of. As now,

    the question

  these crows make of flight,

one wing lifting another, like that,

    like this, her head and mine

  upon the feathered pillow.

33RD ANNIVERSARY OF YARD SALE ROMANCE

When a buck bought your "Time of the Season,"
tick tock, ding dong, brrrring brrrring,
you became the Etch A Sketch drawing me,
the Wiffle ball my bat had lost, and I the kite

you lofted across the day's electric sky.
Because tick tock ding there was war
I platooned green army men and you stacked
blocks whose alphabet spelled our rifled future.

Then you the tabled dishes, mismatched cracked,
you the Denby and Wedgwood, your grandmother's
gilded tea cup even I might be poured in,
one lump or two, sweetened to meet the folks.

By noon's tock you became the sun-faced clock
and I your Ray-O-Vac double A, then you the crock pot
burnt orange and avocado, so I was the dial
turned "Off" or "High" in true Seventies fashion.

Tick bong ding, it was time of the season for loving—
the always-party—so you were the glossy LP
and I the spindle you spun around at 33 1/3,
the needle riding your groove and song.

After dinner you were lavender heather,
paten leather, crinoline, and Irish lace.
When you lit our exotic melancholy,
the patchouli burning in you was me.

Everything was tick ding, brrrring ring,
you the tumbling racks of paperbacks dusting
our Age of Aquarius. You the Romance novel
and I the one bedded to savor your story.

Immigrant Song

The Breckenridge backpack
　　stocks
water, granola, stale trail jerky,
　　and my
garage band broken when the Delco's
　　union jobs
caboosed down Dixie's one-way tracks,
　　whistling bye bye.
There's Donny's lyrics Vox amps feedback
　　black.
Mark's drunken drumming until groupies blink
　　then pony up.
Jerry's flannel fingers, Tom's thumbing long-neck
　　shadows midnight
can't ink. At bottom, there's big-haired me, raking a pick
　　through minor chords.
But here, risen 12,330 cleft feet up Hoosier Ridge, namesake
　　of my escaped-state's
swing-shift fisticuffs, noon's sentimental wind thwacks my jacket,
　　bullies
my cap. Even pica scurry from the human S.O.B. I was in my neck
　　of the woods
when Led Zeppelin clenched its knuckled fist. Back there plink plunk,
　　plunk plink,
music punched my ticket. Dig it, if I'd stayed I'd dug my grave: drunks
　　plying the chemical river,
bread-loaf brick streets, the reeking glue-sniffers' heaven, sticky bailiwick
　　of bacon-faced Bruce
grunting, "Man, you're one mean mo-fo," his tongue black as burnt wick.

In Heaven

There's no clock budget pork presidential tollway
No wrong way off ramp finger horn curse
No median cop no may I see your license
No kid wailing his siren from the dirty diaper car seat
No change exact or perpetual

There's no TPR report no email voice mail text message
No hey didn't you get the memo
No Excel spreadsheet virus hard drive crash
No offshore tech support no please repeat that Vishnu Amran Mehta

There's no cable dish satellite projection TV
No Weight Watchers Lean Cuisine cellulite stretch mark love handles
There's no grass stain no ring around the collar but a halo above thy head
No lemon fresh Tide no reason to Shout it out
No rerun Three's Company but the classic father son and holy ghost

No my friends is heaven's word meaning there's grace but
No grilled bell pepper olive oil garlic basil up there either
No steak baked potato I'm telling you no sour cream cayenne A1
No kiwi banana no apple that started this no-no list

No feta pepperoni black olives no pineapple Canadian bacon
No sleeping beneath windows neon glazed with rain
No dunk three pointer touchdown grand slam around the world
No squeeze bunt organist's "Light My Fire"
No little black dress pearls finger tips so there's God but no *oh oh god*

There's no parsnip asparagus taut hot mustard buttocks listen up
No Moon Mountain cabernet means
No cork to uncork no comma no punctuation of pleasure and that's
No way to live forever or otherwise

No I say say
Yes that feels good I like it may I have some more say
Yes to here and yes upon the lips' now
Yes say
Yes to this finite unzipped uncorked amen

REHEARSAL

What of waking from an afternoon's nap,

      a hand or foot "gone to sleep,"

    dead metaphor not unlike that other.

Then the tingling as does the feather

      of sex delivering its little forever,

    body reborn wearing needle sock or sleeve.

In this we're the audience that never leaves,

      an actor who always acts.

      We laugh, knowing whose line comes next.

You there, at the purple curtain's rope, what of this

      bliss and menace, this applause

    whose pulse thrums first and last.

IN THE NAME OF NAMES

Morning radio announced what events are no-go with snow,
    a Rotary list
ending with Don Downer's "Spiritualism" lecture, postponed
    till late May.
One wonders what the good doctor Downer knows about
    spiritual uplift,
and then, why brook such delay? What's with Whitey's
    really blond hair,
Rusty's freckle picnic, and Mrs. Candy's naming her sweet
    daughter Penny?
What to make of Bob Shovel's arriving home post-blizzard
    to steal
his irascible neighbor's cleared spot, the *Tribune's* headline:
    Robert Shovel Killed by Shovel.

This is what I shovel about, moving here to there
    or there
to here, memory digging incrementally downward
    to my teacher
Mrs. Sweet, you who were anything but. At the rusted tip
    of this shovel
you're grading my color-penciled *Love's Kaleidoscope* a zero,
    sophomoric lyrics
bled upon the teary page as Shelley had, limp wrist upon
    wan forehead.
You're deciding the boy in Honors who doesn't care for
    Eliot
is third period's fraud, "Son, you didn't write these."
    You're right.

I'll admit the Too-Little-Linebacker me didn't, nor the elusive
    Spitball-King.
Ditto my Skip-Church guy, Class-President-Elected-on-a-
    Party-Platform,
the Lucky-Drunk-Cops-Almost-Caught-in-his-Chevy's trunk,
    as well as
Way-Too-Poor-for-Patti's-Daddy and that always zitty
    White-Sprinter-
Black-Guys-Knew-by-Name-and-Time-at-the-City-Meet.
    Wait, Mrs. Not-So-Sweet,
one of me really did pencil that rainbow of love poems!—
    the Raspberry-Beret-Wearing-
Theretofore-Unseen-and-Thereafter-Banished-to-the-Closet
    me.

You're not your name's Sweet, and I'm not the "stone"
    Stein's German implies.
Forgive our selves' their many indiscretions: your sourness,
    my poems'
Sweet & Low. Now you're in a home the kids won't visit,
    I in the path
of a Rocky Mountain boulder sure to plant me poetically
    à la Mr. Shovel.
Let's make our peace before the hymns' graveside shoveling.
    You'll rest beneath
"Sweet" and I beneath a stone with "Stein" redundantly
    carved in it,
our names tragicomic: one pun and a paradox six feet above
    us.

Pilgrim Fortune

When *Mrs.* William Bradford, as ownership went those days,

    spyglassed the New World without steeple or road

  or village square, she death-leapt from the Mayflower's low rail.

Hers a metaphysical question gone aground—absence the pilgrim revelation,

    as was mother's purchasing Masses for my father's

  health and soul. The sale of indulgence gave Luther reason

to nail *Theses* to his church door, though some of Luther's also grounded,

    a notion William understood of the Mrs.

  The rest's a foggy mirror our breath appears to disappear in.

When the Super Bowl party's "free-delivey" Chinese sailed up,

    dinner arrived with a ship bell's ringing my door,

  the guy's car his sloop adrift upon a sea of snow.

Sunday's only certainty was a good tip and cheap chopsticks—

    not unlike the rib Adam loaned to Eve.

  The house floated a crossed-ocean of Asian, black, and honky faces

my colorblind dog could tell apart only by scent or temperament.

Exiles on the lam, holy Dalai Lamas wholly with doubt,

we begged our deliverer, *Master, what of tomorrow?* He bore

no portents, save the fortune cookie my dog swallowed whole.

Sugared fate wended its way through her then out,

the way you and I, dear pilgrims, will lovely exit this world's body.

WET CARPET AWAKENING

Cursing the stubbed-toe 2 AM call—*my father?*—

    I picked up a woman's feather-brushed gush,

    "Wilbur, it's a grandson! Jamaal Jose O'Bryant."

And I, unhappily not Wilbur, croaked *Wrong number* as one does

    when plucked frog-eyed off sleep's lily pad.

    She was old. Who else misdials the pay phone's tiny numbers?

Who else marries a Wilbur, their grandchild an American blend?

    Outside rain misted not cats and dogs but litters of kittens.

    Her lavender sachet apology, my bed-headed threnody,

my *No problem,* and click. Lightning cracked night's black egg

    in halves I couldn't tap back in place:

    My father's dead. I'm next.

Revelation arrives like that, thunder trailing the flash.

    I rode the open window's wet carpet awakening,

    storm flipping its toggle above the wind-blown yarrow,

electric as any newborn. Shaggy, late autumn, nearly gone-to-seed bloom, naked ecstatic.

I floated my trial run out a window the rain had come

in. When the dark made light of me I was.

4

Wrestling Li Po for the Remote

While I recited you, Li Po, *Cops* broadcast
a wife-beater's earning his shirt's eponymous name,
and televised badges arrived to disassociate sign
from signified as did Derrida with nightsticks.

The drama bled so American you changed
channels as the cuffs' half moons first kissed
then swallowed the man's bloody wrists.
You flipped our feathered page, sighing.

Somewhere on Mercy Street the woman's halter
hardly halters what it's meant to. Somewhere
the chapel of her body proposes its commandment,
"Do whatever makes you *less* unhappy."

Somewhere it's plaid boxers and meth-teeth,
filmed behind a trailer's busted screen door.
But our channel's a sparrow perched on branch.
The remote's not under the couch. It's in us.

Your poems lie in my hands, lying. Why is there
nothing of An Lushan's war hounding your heels,
nothing of dead-scalloped streets of sacked Chang'an?
Nothing of exile's knife pressed against your gut.

Instead, you've taught me *wu-wei*, "doing nothing"—
the way a mountain floats its own cloud river,
these blossoms flute their yellow-petaled tune,
the universe unfolding its fist within us.

That's why I repeated "somewhere" three times
in five lines to distance the daily perfidy
as you did by ignoring it—anaphora my faux Tao.
Students of Zen don't abide boozy wifebeaters.

No, a blind eye's the remote's remote,
as is one's head slung upon the limned wind.
You fell drunken into a river and drowned,
trying to embrace the moon. I drowned in you.

Old master, I'm done. I've pulled the plug
on my dead man's float, I've clicked off
the sparrow's song. Now where's that knife?
Where's your chest, these eyes plucked that I may see.

ARTS ELEVATED AND OTHER

"Afghanistan's my generation's classic,
          like your Beatles, or this fat chick."
     The soldier hoisted his prosthetic arm toward
Vermeer's *The Milkmaid*, rousing a passel of gallery guards
          from arm-crossed iPod nod-off.
     He shot straight. Lucky Vermeer's fleshy lass
makes unlikely vixen beside our model-waif's collar bones.
          She dribbles milk from a pitcher's *oh*,
     pearls before the coming orgasmic splash.
But who's the luckiest Beatle?
          Shut up, his art fired, glinting off
     the guards' gilded plastic badges, the shushed crowd
giving peace a chance. That she's already *melken* the cow
          suggests she'd yank a man's attention in the hay,
     the way Cupid's wingéd song ends always
with yeah-yeah-yeah then self-hate.
          George, the quiet one?
     That's bull, his art spouted, twist and shout
parsed symphonic on the lips of his sergeant shot dead.
          Stravinsky said the violins of his "Soldier's Tale"
     speak beyond "the realm of verbal meanings,"
as did The Beatles' rooftop last concert—skyward
          implying the elevation of art and play
     if not the end of both. Even Mendelssohn believed
idea poured from music's pitcher into the pink bowl of his ear
          "too definite to be put into words."
     Can't we just let it be?
His art motored, *Screw you, old man,*
          humming engine running,
     he alone in the door-down garage
of his Dantean hometown.
          In dotage Langer claimed music's

     "a tonal analogue of emotive life,"
our full-throttled taxi anthem heading uptown.
        The joke's not Ringo.
    but any man who'll argue drivel
though not the assorted wars of his moment.

A Brief History of History

Herodotus, the Father of,
fashions it of chit chat and the dilly dally.
Now ours Benzedrine-buzz-rush throttles up,
all interstate and no rest stops.

Three centuries post-Vermeer's *The Milkmaid*,
the '57 Chevy's our classic beauty. Undaunted
by spilt milk, Levi-Strauss says it's unified
because we "choose, sever, and carve it up,"

so Cupid flitting behind the Maid's behind
writes her back story. The lucky one's cup runneth
over, double D. The rest shift a stripped gearbox,
gaskets blown not halfway home.

Von Ranke claims it's the big story
of "what actually happened."
Try that line on your gray professor—
or the cops. Mostly it goes backwards

while motoring ahead, the two-faced Janus.
Walter Benjamin suggests there's an Angel of,
though devilish Nietzsche laments those
"eunuchs who guard the historical harem."

In theory, these lies we lie to lie together.
In application, the backseat's where it happens
to most of us most of the time,
milked thus shut up. In sum, whoever's

at the wheel inserts his key then drives—
meaning the news is not the wreck
but who tells that story: a sere crust
ringing the milk cup of what is.

Keeping Score

The Professional Bowlers Association rode the groove
    of Sixties TV,
blissful Chris Schenkel whispering above sugar-footed
    Dick Weber's approach
and delivery, his weekend job to throw strikes knocking
    assembled pins
and not the noggins of union strikers in want of.

Songwriters parsed a simpler time, suggesting all-white
    and polyester,
their ruse using fewer words to score the Top Ten,
    averaging
merely 176 *sans* articles. Now lyricists spew 435 to say less
    digitally,
zeroes and ones not unlike the digits fingers make when

rolling a ball down polished wood at a triangle built
    to be exploded.
Strike and explode converged as sentence-act in smokey
    bowling alleys,
grass huts, and Viet Cong tunnels as calm-as-ever-Weber
    won 36 tournaments,
drying his hand upon the air jet's insouciant comfort.

Networks' handful we counted with one and thumb leftover,
    leftovers warming
our oven as Schenkel gushed physical intimacies of the 6-10
    split
and 8 of 12 Sha Na Na bandmates earned advanced degrees
    after playing
Woodstock, its muddied crowd wondering what the.

The nation believed in nation—if one overlooked riots,
    who got shot,
and those suffocating on vomit—so men conceived
    bowling leagues
to flee Tuesday's dollhouse. Everybody knew everybody
    if only because
the cursive shirts bore their names, my father's stitched *Joe*.

Teams posed for pictures with hands on their freshly
    polished balls,
season's average displayed in red digits at their ever
    expanding waists,
his cracking 188 because the nation believed in
    upward mobility
the way one's score might rightly rise by dint of.

In memory my father's enthroned upon Olympus,
    slinging thunderbolt
laughter and The Great Society. The Lion in Winter
    was he,
my unshaven minister of pre-cable Sunday afternoons.
    It's no wonder
23% of Brits believe Churchill's a mythical figure.

He hauled me out to practice being a man among men
    by wearing
another's shoes. I waded feet in their microbial miasma,
    fingering
the ball's moist holes before I'd learned a woman's secrets
    or my own.
Now 20% of French men admit to being "uninterested in sex."

For them *ennui* has wracked the aging balls of our sexual
    revolution,

brie more appealing than. In America 69% of Republicans
        believe in
the prospect of hell, though notably none among the denizens
        of Antartica's
McMurdo Station, who deplaned with 12,132 condoms

to service the winter of their content. That chilly McMurdo
        sports
a bowling alley, but France has so few, posits reason to pine for
        the *Great Bowling Revival*.
Back then, my father believed hard work gets one ahead,
        as do a surprising
71% of US Muslims—quaint faith amid our darkening alleys.

ODE TO CANDY BARR, FIFTIES' STAG QUEEN

Bowling teams fibbed

    to the beehived wives,

  polished balls safe

    in their zippered bags.

Before the second reel

     they'd spun Candy Barr puns,

  "I'd like to ____ her wrapper,"

    "I'd nibble her creamy _____."

Candy flickered across motel walls,

    her ample nipples pierced by

  picture hooks. Dust haloed the room

    then her.

CAT CHURCH COMMUNION

Because Cubby lives in the vapid attic
Rev. Jim Jones rented pre-Kool-Aid rampage,
we drank cheap wine from Dixie cups.
We think this is funny. Never mind the tenses.
Cubby's not his real name, everything disguised
to protect the guilty. He's reciting olde English,
window as well as mirror of *were* and *are* and *will be.*
Dead's the answer but not yet. Dean Young's
heart is still young, pumping irony pre-transplant,
he flat upon the shag speaking Mandarin
to a Siamese cat. No, the cat's reciting Li Po,
fellow drunk whose name's not changed
to protect the innocent. It's here the Rev
resolved, *Never again will I be poor for Jesus!*
A picture window brushstrokes the alley's
sprung bedsprings and a trash can spilling
our Chinese last supper the cat got,
speaking her alley cat high Mandarin.
Breaking bread, Jesus knew something
would go wrong for us but opted hands off,
we know not what we do. Providence
is named Steve, or was, before Cubby,
who claims puddles make blue eyes of sky
when viewed from above, meaning they
mirror the divine if one was looking down.
Or is. Shaggy Dean's heart is broken
in the literal and soon to be figurative sense,
though he doesn't know it or even how
the not-yet ex will rip his out then how
Dr. L. plumbed another's in, its beat
not stilled by that horizontal Harley.
Never mind the tenses. Kids play soccer

five stories beneath our feet. Everything's
beneath our feet: Jim Jones, his punch drunk
followers, the Congressman all in the ground.
Or become it. Cubby thinks this is fun and so
does that cat who's neither. The ball rolls
its muddy dead head from one foot to another,
the kid gods deciding who gets it, who not.
Soon enough it's us, the paper cup empty.
Now the Rev's pretty kitty figure-eights
our blue-jeaned shins, purring Mandarin.
Her tag's big red heart says she's named "Luv,"
alive because he abandoned her. Or it.

Is Beautiful

Black is the new blonde, so everyone wants a piece
    in these halcyon days
when politics makes oh-so-hot what heretofore
    had borne
the mark of Cain, or at least sufficient cause to get
    one's head
civil-rights-clubbed by a jowly Southern sheriff
    chewing tobacco
once harvested by wagonloads of slaves. No more
    Get to the back
of the bus, boy. No more *boy*. Black is the new blonde.

Now septuagenarian Larry King smugly proclaims
    his young son
yearns to be black, announcement to crystallize
    the social leap
from racism right through the color-blindedness
    we never attained
to an elevated plateau where black smacks cool.
    All's better now.
No more dumb blonde jokes, "Tell me, how many
    blondes
does it take to screw a low watt light bulb?"

No more "a priest, a rabbi, and a black guy walked
    into a bar . . ."
jokes that flashed a match of stifled laughter
    as well as guilt
easily blown out, right index pantomiming
    no, no, no
in the smokey white air. Black is the new blonde.
    When Alphonso Toss

secret-knocked me through the Soul Hole's 1974 door,
    I was neither black
nor blond. Roosevelt Johnson and His Seven Seas

milked a wet-silk blues set, uh-huh, black faces
    in tidal sway.
Eyeing me, the collective Seven Seas stilled mid-howl
    because I is white.
"Brothers," Alphonso lilted, "this cat's with me,"
    so Roosevelt unfurled
his stalled growl while a stand-up bass cleaned what
    muddy break
my skin had wrought. The answer's three blondes:
    one to screw
and two to brush her shoulder-length hair.

What would Emmett Till think of Larry's white tot's
    pining for an afro,
Emmett not-so-breezily swinging from that crooked tree?
    What Medgar, Martin,
and Clayton, my knifed-dead friend? Has Jackie Robinson
    slid home safe at last?
Citizens, we want so badly what we want to believe,
    clink clink.
No more Shines, the robed choir sings, *No more Sambo*—
    while history's solo,
unswayed amidst all this swaying, whistles Dixie.

Parable of America in Four-Part Harmony

*I say we had best look our times . . . searchingly in
the face, like a physician diagnosing some deep disease.*
—Walt Whitman / "Democratic Vistas"

1 / The Soup Compromise

Some say soup's the food kingdom's model
Marxist, giving freely of itself in service
to the greater good. Its stovetop ethic:
From each onion according to its pungency,
to each zucchini according to its blandness.
Others say soup's secret recipe brings
capitalism to boil with a dash of Adam
Smith's "enlightened self-interest."

Monetary policy bubbles to mush in soup lines
meant to feed the masses thus squelch revolt,
though spoons of Russian caviar and our T-bone
steak make suitable weapons for attacking
the pilot's cabin. Safety *and* profit induced airlines
to nix free lunch but charge for luggage,
the captains of industry banking our hygienic
gamble: Pack clean underwear or Febreze?

That cleanliness *is* a kind of greed makes
Marxism appealing in theory if not practice
when showering becomes one's political choice.
Strange how spreading the commune's manure
across freshly tilled fields predicts in odor
and outcome the untidy work of a faculty
senate, the steaming residue of goats
and English profs feeding seedlings' roots.

What comes of such work earns many names,
hyphenates that fatten slim books and fuel
students' worldly hunger. In soup circles
the thicker its name the thicker the end product,
chowder eventually giving way to stews
eaten with a fork. Not unlike my colleague's
changing names to pass as faux ethnic,
soup's AKA goulash, gumbo, consommé,

potage, bouillabaisse, and boring old broth
the favored diet of famished fashion models.
Simply making soup blends opposites like Dems
and the GOP—as does an atom, as does
my risking English profs and fashion models
in the same poem. Ponder cover girls, senators,
and the tenured all ensconced in a DC kitchen,
stainless steel buffering their unifying polarity.

Easy to see who's the proton, positively lovely.
Even simpler to cipher who's shouldering electron
negativity and who's carrying no charge at all.
What's composed by this convergence let's call
"citizenry"—the collaboration of opposing forces
not a mode of bipartisan resentment
in the manner of Congress, or anthrax.
Too many cooks don't spoil the broth.

If impunity implies a bully's getting away with
something—say, China's censoring Google,
those BofA bailouts, deniable incursions into
and out of the cracked Iraq of another's heart—
the Soup Compromise suggests middle ground.

Let's bring tribal give and take to simmer
not boil, stirring Walt's big American pot:
the word given body—negotiation's creation.

In this effort well-balanced soup proffers
useful lessons in cooperation and tanginess.
Let's ladle a steaming tutorial bowl
and share the cupboard's silver spoons.
Let's dine outside the velvet ropes
and dab our lips with the paper napkin
of our need, risking the day's poisons.
Let's spice our soup with peppered yeses.

2 / Negotiating the Global Economy

My Middle Kingdom, population 1,
begins each day with pushups, sit ups,
and reflections on capitalism as fashioned
by AIG and BofA. Then coffee and toast.
BofA reminds me in behavior and sound
of MoFo, acronym black comics
drop on the show's paying audience
and white boys spout to bag their baggy jeans.

BofA metaphorically MoFoed my mother,
donuting her only stock down to zero
as object lesson to the meddling poor.
MoFo's Oedipal thus Greek
though instantly understandable
on the blacktop basketball court
where I first heard and used it,
jacking jump shots and talking smack.

Thanks to Google, MoFo's as global as BofA,
rattling China's cage of Confucianism and
cheap credit. *Informational imperialism* MoFoes
Mao's little red book, Google threatening
obedience to authority as did missionary-
astronomer Adam Schall's blending of
Copernicus and the Bible. He MoFoed
the Chinese imperial court circa 1661,

aligning its stars with Christian heaven—
Jesus loves you. Now hand over your silk.
As the church profits from marketable souls,
the state prefers hymns sung with unthinking
social harmony, so the mandarins silenced

Schall by strangulation—an ironic verdict
halted only when thunder persuaded
his judges that nature's gods disagreed.

The morning's toast and coffee signal resignation
to the worldly body as well as to the world's body
whose atlas of power resides in others' hands.
This geography of weakness inks our fate
as did the calfskin maps Matteo Ricci unrolled
before the stunned Chinese, back when
the Middle Kingdom believed itself the center
of our planet, as did I in adolescence.

Today's shallow chit chat dials our social contract
between poles of hermeticism and global citizenry.
It's either porn's topographics or prayers for Tibet.
Here, my morning's web headline touts the pure
Confucian logic China applies to censor Google—
flashing the Middle Kingdom's middle finger.
Now, the digitized news of how we got screwed
by BofA's pinstriped MoFos.

3 / T P

The Barons of American Toilet Paper
possessed the splinterless genius—
finessed as well our nation's sacrificial pines
and the five Great Lakes to ferry
their saleable goods pre- and post-

production. In America cleanliness
is next to godliness, as is free enterprise
at root and demise, in whose solemn
service the Northern Tissue Co. employs
thousands to make cash of our sodden

waste. Money can be spun from anything,
even what disgusts us. Say, the Kardashians?
Splinterless means we cleanse our collective
ample bobos, bottoms, rears, and asses
without the old days' leaf or cloth,

without corn cob, catalog, or Afghani's
smooth stone—without even Bidet's
spritzing. In public the restroom's lonely
for reason. When there's a crowd
in there, look out!—someone's getting

arrested. In school the nuns shuttled us
to the *lavatory,* our necessary deed
as vile as the devil they'd not wed
in favor of pretty Jesus nailed to the cross,
also arrested but alone. To feel at home

experts advise fraidy-cat lecturers:
"Imagine your audience naked!"

Better to imagine the crowd enthroned pants
down, all the powerful or the merely pouty
reduced to TP duty. This, Freud theorized,

is our elemental art: the holy mess we make
making ourselves our first creation!
On white paper, and in the body of truth,
the essential human experiment is always
to become something else—or to be

nothing at all. Take heart, my friends.
We are citizens of a universal movement.
Through us a galactic give-and-take recycles
our carbon, the cosmos unrolling the perfect
charm of its perforated symmetry.

4 / Organizational Theory

Alphabetizing means if one's Adams
only Abel or the occasional aardvark
keeps one from the front of the line.
But Williams, Young, and Zwank
can wet their pants.

The system freezes the chill waters
of American capitalism in totalitarian ice,
and there's no melting pot up or down
that line, comrade, unless lucky Lola Zeller
marries her way up to Mrs. Robert Charles.

That's sexism, an organizational mode,
as is racism—ghettos and country clubs
keeping things in their proper places, say,
the working poor and bankers whose wives
tie sweaters around their pink necks.

For some in America it's a Vail chalet,
for others there's Flint's kiss my ass,
wealth as numerical as the Dewey decimal's
stoic way—poetry here, architecture there—
all the overlooked art and cookbooks

relegated to the unlit basement. There,
at least one's hospitably grouped among
those sharing interest in goulash or
Kandinsky, unlike school's seating chart
where Adams mostly pulls Abel's pigtails.

In America, behind the velvet rope's
sniffling maitre d', exclusivity's a function

of who can't get in—as are borders
and the Ivy League. Organization aspires
to purity (a measure of what's not there).

It hates democracy's sloppy kitchen,
preferring tidy-up's broom and social dustpan.
But the soup culture cooks is *us*, remaking
recipes that make us anew—we the risen
citizenry, reorganizing the organization.

A pinch of change seasons the gumbo of power.
Witness my town's *Space Cowboy*, steps rising like
butterflies to milkweed bloom, guiding patients
to the liberty of pot under glass—freedom's meds
arrayed from Alhambra Lift Off to Zanzibar Paradise.

Workers on the Fifth Street Overpass

From below the Fifth Street overpass I looked up through
    my sun roof's open hole
then through the hole men pointed at. This, how America works.
    Up top, a black guy
leaned on his tool, the shovel job in union hierarchy fathomed best
    if one's dues-paying,
as once I was but am no longer in any formal sense. I've worked
    a little with a shovel.
There's the hole dug then planted. There's a hole filled then driven
    over, walked on, knelt beside.
Reader, you've worked a little too, if not the shovel's conscience
    then the cash register's ding-ding,
the boss's coffee, a screw's twisted insistence whizzing down line
    as did my homefront mother,
while hubby dug a boggy Aleutian hole with an army green shovel,
    his hovel of a house
lovely when bullets were about, there where the sun hung looking
    down all night.

From below I looked up through the hole men pointed at as if
    someone had spilled from heaven
or risen up from hell. I hoped to see my dead dad, winking back,
    traffic stalled
on our Grecian urn. Instead, it was the hole's eye I looked through
    thinking oh how poetic
when the black guy reappeared with shovels over his shoulders
    like glittering wings.
Simile lifted off the Fifth Street overpass, his work now mine.
    When the overalled angel
bent on dirty knee, looking down, a circle of fists and handles,
    he nodded at me

the way men do when passing in alleys, unarmed but dangerous.
    Sun haloed him
with Jim Crow. The overpass wrapped me in Black Panther fists.
    This, how America works.
I nodded through the hole hanged like our dead century between
    us.

Acknowledgments

Several poems in this book appeared previously. Grateful acknowledgment is made to the following publishers: *Arts & Letters PRIME*: "Sputnik Summer." *Boulevard*: "Cardinal Numbers: Sequence in which No One Dies" and "Field Guide." *Cape Rock*: "Ars Poetica @ 59," "Forgiven," and "The Soup Compromise." *Colorado Review*: "6 Chair's Lift Line, Breckenridge." *Connotation Press: An Online Artifact*: "33rd Anniversary of Yard Sale Romance," "Cat Church Communion," "Immigrant Song," "*Night Visit to the Recycling Center*, a Three-Album Box Set," "Parable of the Sentence." and "Wrestling Li Po for the Remote." *Crab Orchard Review*: "To Illinois's Gold Star Mothers, Who Lost a Child to War." *Fifth Wednesday Journal*: "Antiphon for Les Paul," "Is Beautiful," and "Workers on the Fifth Street Overpass." *Fourth River*: "Upon Seeing, in Shadow, a Red Tail Hawk Plunder the Song Bird's Nest." *Hamilton Stone Review*: "In the Name of Names." *The Laurel Review*: "Blind Voyeur" and "In Heaven." *New Ohio Review*: "Wet Carpet Awakening." *The North American Review:* "A Brief History of History." *The Peorian*: "Son Room." *Poetry East*: "Sunrise, Snowfall, Two Crows among Lodgepole Pines." *Poetry Northwest:* "Rehearsal." *Shenandoah*: "Apple Trees at Petal Fall with Li Po." *Sou'wester*: "Arts Elevated and Other" and "In the Interest of Brevity, Let's Begin at the End." "The Afterlife" appeared in *An Endless Skyway: Poems from the Poets Laureate of the United States* (Ice Cube Press, 2011).

For sage advice and welcome support, I am indebted especially to David Wojahn. Thanks as well to Susan Hahn, Beckian Fritz Goldberg, Bob Hicok, Donald Revell, Jeff Knorr, Dean Young, Jeff Gundy, Clint McCown and Keith Ratzlaff. Thanks also to Crowe, Fuller, and Teeven. Thanks to *Jimmy's* for scores and highlights. Thanks to Miss Tiger Lily Delight for lighting beauty's fuse. Thanks to Deb without whom there is none. Thanks to Kirsten and Joseph for the gifts of themselves. I'm grateful also to Bradley University for granting me time to write many of these poems.

"The Good Dog's Valentine Cento" is dedicated to Lily. "Today I Was Happy, So I Made This Poem" is for Annie Wright, in memory of James.

FIFTH STAR PRESS is an independent, not-for-profit publishing house devoted to Chicago's publishing past, present, and future. For information about our titles, our mission, how to submit, or how to donate, please visit our website, www.fifthstarpress.org.